magic kingdom through my eyes

NICK MENCHACA

AuthorHouse™
1663 Liberty Drive
Bloomington, IN 47403
www.authorhouse.com
Phone: 833-262-8899

Because of the dynamic nature of the Internet, any web addresses or links contained
in this book may have changed since publication and may no longer be valid. The views
expressed in this work are solely those of the author and do not necessarily reflect the
views of the publisher, and the publisher hereby disclaims any responsibility for them.

Any people depicted in stock imagery provided by Getty Images are models,
and such images are being used for illustrative purposes only.
Certain stock imagery © Getty Images.

This book is printed on acid-free paper.

ISBN: 978-1-6655-6391-8 (sc)
ISBN: 978-1-6655-6392-5 (e)

Library of Congress Control Number: 2022912165

Print information available on the last page.

Published by AuthorHouse 07/15/2022

authorHOUSE®

Dedication Page:

This book is dedicated to all Autistic kids
who see things a little differently!

The magic of the Disney journey through the eyes of an autistic boy. This journey of Disney is the happiest place on Earth, and it started when I was 3 years old.

However, I didn't really understand how much Disney World meant to me until we moved to Orlando, 20 minutes from Disney World. I was not a fan of large crowds when I was younger, they made me feel scared because of all the loud noises.

Years later I still have a difficult time with crowds. Now, our first stop inside Magic Kingdom is the stroller rental counter. Being in the stroller helps me to handle the large crowds. Once we receive my stroller, we are headed to City Hall to pick up our magic cards.

The magic cards allow you to cast spells all throughout the park. This is fun to do because you get to solve clues to make the magic work, which is something I love to do!

Next, we turn the corner, and we are headed into the park. My mom pushes my stroller down Main Street U.S.A. toward Cinderella's Castle. I begin to take in the smells, sights, and sounds.

All of a sudden, I hear the ragtime music from the speakers and quickly pull my hands up to cover my ears. When I was 18 months old my mom took me to an audiologist who said I had hypersensitive hearing. This means that I hear everything at a higher decimal than most other people. Therefore, loud noises, are difficult for me, especially in crowded places.

My mom notices and hands me my safety net...my noise canceling headphones. Little did I know that these headphones would be what helped me to be able to tolerate the loud noises.

Around the next corner in Adventureland, I watch different characters pose for photos with guests. I desperately want to meet these characters.

My favorite character is Goofy because he always has fun. With my headphones in toe, I head to Goofy to get my picture. What an amazing feeling! I tell my mom one day I want to work at Disney as a character.

After my picture, we are headed to Fantasyland. As we get closer and closer, I start to smell the freshly popped popcorn. The taste of Disney popcorn is the best in the World!

With our popcorn in hand my mom and I head into the Country Bear Jamboree, but not before she hands me my headphones. The animatronic singing bears get me up on my feet clapping to the beat.

After leaving the Country Bear Jamboree, we head towards Liberty Square. Here I get to ride the Haunted Mansion. As I enter, I'm a little nervous of the dark space and loud sounds, but once inside the magic of the Mansion captures my attention and my fears are gone.

Upon exiting the Haunted Mansion ride, we are headed toward one of my favorite attractions, Mickeys Philharmagic concert in Fantasyland. This adventure messes with all your senses...but in a good way! Throughout the experience you smell fresh pies, feel the water when the mops are cleaning the mess in the kitchen, and you hear the rushing of the wind as you fly through the sky on a magic carpet.

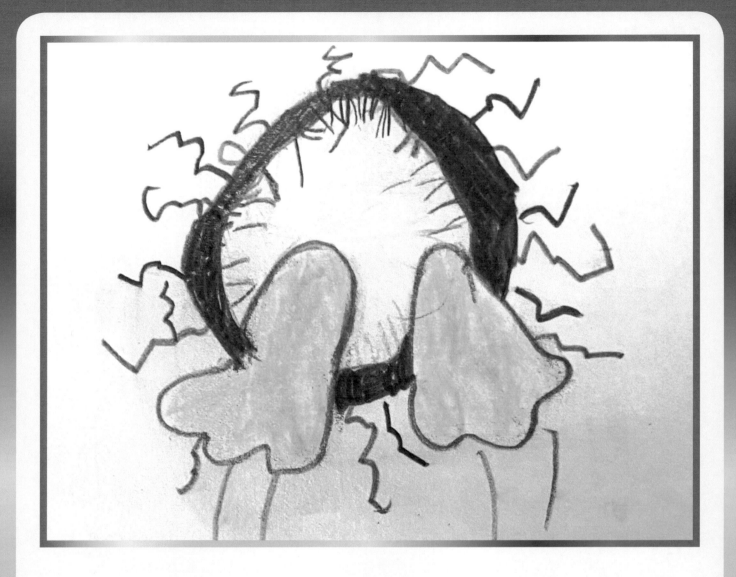

As much as I love this concert, I must put my headphones on to be able to immerse myself into adventure of Mickeys Philharmagic concert.

Unfortunately, at the end of the concert Donald is stuck in the wall.

We are now headed off to our next stop, Tomorrowland. On our way there I hear a loud boom and look up into the sky to see the most beautiful lights in the sky. The fireworks were going off over the castle to signal the end of a character performance. They are very loud but extremely beautiful!

The magic of Disney once again puts a smile on my face. I see every little detail of the sparkle in the sky that the fireworks have to offer. Next, we zoom into the Speedway, and I smell gasoline in the air. I beg my mom to stop so we can drive the cars. The noise is loud, but ole faithful, my headphones, will get me through the ride!

As we drive, I have a sense of freedom. I am the driver of my destiny, and I can go anywhere I want to go. We finally come to a stop, and we hop off, head up the stairs and out to our next destination which is the Carousel of Progress.

Carousel of Progress here we come! This is by far my favorite attraction at the park! It's a slow-moving ride that doesn't have loud noises. This ride allows me to relax and enjoy the attraction without having to use my headphones. This attraction shows me what the past looked like and what a great big, beautiful tomorrow has in store for us!

It's time to head home, but as my mom and I start to head back to Main Street USA we stop one more place, Plaza Ice Cream Parlor. It has the best vanilla ice cream on the planet! I know that sounds plain, but I don't like anything on my ice cream, just plain vanilla tastes the best to me.

Now looking back on my visit to Disney World, I realize, there is only one feeling that describes the awe you experience entering the parks - happiness.

Being with your family and friends, it's wonderful to create memories that are so magical. This place sparks a delight and joy that only Disney can provide! Everyone's journey in Magic Kingdom is different, but on my journey, it is so magical. Being an autistic boy didn't change a thing on how awesome the Disney Magic makes everyone feel.

Printed in the United States
by Baker & Taylor Publisher Services